I am the tallest animal in the world.

1

I am the largest bird in the world,
but my wings are too small for fly-
ing, so I run instead.

My funny name means "river horse." I am not a horse, but I do spend lots of time in the water.

I am the largest animal living in the water.

I live in the sea, always carry a shell
and lay my eggs on a sandy beach.

I do not drink, because I get everything I need from the eucalyptus leaves I eat.

I have a hump on my back and like to live in deserts.

I have sharp teeth and gnaw down
trees to build dams in ponds.

When I am in danger, I give off an awful smell to scare away my enemies.

I am the biggest animal that lives on land.

I can run faster than any other
animal.

I eat insects and am covered with
bony plates that protect me.

At one time, millions of my ances-
tors roamed America and Indians
would hunt me.

I have two very long teeth called tusks.

I am black and white and furry. I
love to eat bamboo.

When I am a baby, I have a tail.
When I grow older, I lose my tail
and grow a pair of hind legs.